I0755939

FINISHING LINE PRESS
www.finishinglinepress.com

sample.spring

poems by

Margaret LeMay

Finishing Line Press
Georgetown, Kentucky

sample.spring

ISBN 979-8-89990-361-8 First Edition

Publisher: Leah Huete de Maines
Editor: Christen Kincaid
Cover Art: Margaret LeMay
Author Photo: Miles Lewis
Cover Design: Elizabeth Maines McCleavy

Order online: www.finishinglinepress.com
also available on amazon.com

Author inquiries and mail orders:
Finishing Line Press
PO Box 1626
Georgetown, Kentucky 40324
USA

Contents

driving darkness, a telestich

weak sun slung lowered,
across the interstate and longer
than i'd envisioned it would go. i
felt in the silence a former luv,
luv, lub. january clocks in flux. i
followed my instruction
as i heard it, as articulated turning
somewhat south toward
forest and eventually the river, a
demarcation splitting this
state and the next. the years a tick
and clip, an empty swing in
an opaque dark. now see me
in headlights over rumble strips,
vibration, stars, the empty fields

A matter of words

When I said I wanted what the heart breaks
into, not that the heart breaks into, I should
have insisted. Erase years of talking,
make them gone. White poinsettias go on sale.
Wet snow weighs branches until its pressure's
lifted. Either way. Each era shows a new one.
What the heart breaks into is not at all
the same as breaking into. How snow falls
beneath floodlights, drifts on the bench
where a child's sodden, wadded shirt has stayed
shapeless for weeks. The shirt's gone under.
The plows shake weighted streets. Waiting for
someone who's not coming makes why the heart
extracts itself. The heavy snow keeps falling.

The dreams with a hand hovering above

the cold metal knob, stuck
core bits bore papery wind—
too late, too far to go back and the gray
comes once a day here and
the salt froth in the frozen
light is both a wave and a when
does motion become
when does emotion become
paper light at the end. A hiss of refilling
or sinking. Glass bottle
crashing the bin, the eyes are
the tender. Who can fault the fat
red chest of the cardinal, returning to find
the empty grate, remembering once
here there was feed.

Open the shades. Open to the frigid blue and the steam the house

gives that catches its glass. The leaks in the casements are so
when I sleep and wake the floorboards ache, when small splinters
catch the white blanket. The miles are magnets. Sun casts
on the round table, company backlit here, once, and what if one
day the stalking stops. If one day more becomes clear: a branch
grazing the head, smoke curling, bottles swallowing
the table grate whole, a left-side molar enamel cracked to
the pulp where rice sugar sticks, pulling pain to the full-on
this is. This is company in seeking salvation. The ring in a red clasp
in a steel box now, in the bright sun and cold pavement.
What set by it, went by it. With dry eyes and dry skin.
Perfect light in a closed drawer. Unbroken sky where what clouds
strung up and pulled in. This new softness, the lines
etching smooth tile and his curved belly glistening.
Bathwater runs off his small body. Cold is out there, past
the broken shades, the alley, and the roofline hooded with snow.

In these two degrees, fighting dead gears

and fake grace. Why not just say
I belong when invited. Mottled light
back glow on warbled glass shows
the smudge of skin in the shower
before it at night. This is no privacy,
someone watching the shape
of unclothed under the frozen
silence the house is in the dark
within. Listen. Like the draft is
a window pane, broken, poly, entirely
dislodged from the wood frame which is
itself loose in the opening. Splintered.
Hand to the wood, inadvertently sets
energy forth: sputters all manners.
My child, with his small hands unfolded,
loose, where I lay.

---

sample.spring

I.

Wakes, stumbles the haze out of—
To observe an understanding that—
Stamping on the scraped deck, a singular furred fungus—
To sit, shoulder to shoulder and misunderstand—
To open the curtains, to let light. Sun—
Good night and sweet dreams—
An hour's adjustment forward is—
The kitchen is filled with scorched skillets.—
When I feared the brakes would fail—
The roads gape potholes—
When all is as it should be webs,—
Lint clots on the floor the stopped—

Wakes, stumbles the haze out of

routine borne not of need
but aloneness, an algorithm, a furnace
of switches and clicks, footfall
and rose clippings. Wakes at a voice
that is missing, turning his small face
from the photo, from that which
lacks words. Wildflowers are knots
at the side of the road, chokes
in the throat, tensions in the stomach.
Decals on the wall with petals
poised, posed, cast to be
perpetually falling. Who are you,
there in the roses, when the sounds
are crashing the night.

To observe an understanding that

places registries amid efficiency
needs, wants, the naked gesturing
allowing our presence while fortifying
position. Assumption's a funeral. To gather
what suits, by the convincing brick paneling,
the cut-down and built-in. Belonging in two
places and to neither. An in-between,
an aging village in a silent swath of
flowers and overgrown mines. A barking,
a pounding of footfall, a barely voiced
posturing coiled to strike.

Stamping on the scraped deck, a singular furred fungus

growing out from the siding and the grapes overhead heavy,
splitting skins with green flesh.
Dust from the graveled alley and crooked
stone walls. Waiting there, red-faced.
Why are we not answering the door,
mama. That it would have been different,
hearing each step and speaking
the truth of it, yelling that it
was a slamming car door, a gesture,
obscenities can see you in
cans popping close by in the dark.
Turned down once, insistent
like footfall gathering strength
in its sense of insult, sense harmed,
sense denial. To reassert, to determine.
A blood-warm place I've crawled into.
And tight little arms. Stay,
mama. Stay for some more hours.

To sit, shoulder to shoulder and misunderstand

the puzzle, the terms, the question.
Years reveal veins. But shoulder to
shoulder, attempt. And to rest,
bare branches and hands clasped.
A snow-damp street under gray
sky makes an irregular intersection,
skewed, lining a sidewalk up with
the bridge, the letters, scratched
in the bus shelter bench, light muted
through panels. Short legs swinging
and in the near-distance, a brick campus.
He says it doesn't look like much of
a school. Colorless, the creek
pulse is an ice layer with dark
spots and frail matter within.

To open the curtains, to let light. Sun

breaking blinds. To spread
them at midnight, trading being backlit
for what's out there not knowing
the hour we wake. To let light is
how an animal stirs, distracts, diverts
view from its tracks, blurring
motions and marks of its presence.
Sun on a white wall, frozen stars
overhead from the mattress and dark
masking where exactly here mirrors.

Good night and sweet dreams

are a glow from the kitchen
of built-in shelves too small to hold
miniature benches, a park missing
trees and its lamppost and the fierce
need to stand head nestled in neck, to protect
the short legs and dark eyes through
elements, through roofs and division.
Stroll and sweep, stroll and water
asserts presence and payment,
compensation and cracked frames.
Meals blend one to the next for him,
the same bread each time and rain moving
on and into the sky beyond.

A clear line where water sheeted
from the eavestroughs, where dye cut
the white of the roots. In my dream
you were there visiting me, mama,
small fingers, curled in the
warm rooms that stop being
so in his absence, gentle in
the cloud of its residual cast.

An hour's adjustment forward is

a dream when they tear a chain from
a smaller boy's neck, wrenching paper
cranes into bits. Bolts, bits, scatters
the pavement, stuck and catching
on yellowing bushes. When hands
pull at worn clothing with a name
sewn in and label it trash. Water drips
in the basin and deer fur collects
where plants grasp. Bloodstains
darken the interstate.

The kitchen is filled with scorched skillets.

A different day, it is bare. Light filtering
in through the skylights. Worrying that
hurt has been done when the refusal
to reach out abrades the skin, cuts
to the toe bone, wild parsnip boils picked
to drain in the sunlight. The physical pain
is a high, wavering voice from the dark.
Why are we not answering the door.
A water stain on the silence. Caked mud
brushed off into dust. To call and call out
names, exclusions, how drawn lines ward
off, keep out. How lines mark breaking.
The doorways here are taller and narrower.
Scant room to run, that the floor's hard,
that the rugs' slip is presence gone home.

When I feared the brakes would fail

to engage, it fit holds and sounds of a limbed
season, its stomach of snow
melt amassing silt fractals, refractions. Within
tears that rise, thinking he would let us be,
would let the body transport
the stained bandages
between this era
and the next one be, curled under a desk,
fitting the shadows that were.

The roads gape potholes

the cold broke. To be smiling still
in the smoke and dense fog, in the raw face of
wind, mile markers tracking the white line
curve that is the sole trace in haze
and particulate matter. Pallets and crates
stacked in lots cast the milk plant and a sweet
electricity of sugar and heat. A florescent light
the green signs reflect, emerging one by one,
a hanging with no landscape surrounding.
A woman on the billboard by the curve of the bridge.
Water risen near to its underbelly, words
marked on the concrete, a rupture of
shots, and measures of what one would prefer
not to touch, would rather not mine.

When all is as it should be webs,

nests, a mouthful of tiny pearl teeth, driven
rot in between eight of them, indulgence
born when those grown
never developed such rot, because their own
brushed until we cried.
To have gone wrong. To have
a house with no table impressing
this moment in his thus-far five years,
and there are any number
of somethings painful at the edge,
the lip, the horizon where the trees
are as time makes neighborhoods into
where we lived once, living as
this will move on, will
carry you, will is in many manners right
now showing itself and its blood.

Lint clots on the floor the stopped

drain soaks with soaped
water. The break where the throat
chords breath I found
and gathered, stilled, released.
Gray and gray the house is in the rain
webs over bottles, what it feels
like to see blood from a hard shell
scratching the tender. Mama but I am
fine, even as mama is dry fingers
splitting in many places to bandage.

Wells, swallows. To stare
is the start, a shout gives an electrical
shock, fosters a forever state of turning
one's back to the walls, windows, and doors.
Explains gravity well enough,
on command in the dark.

---

sample.spring

II.

Oak leaves and early spring clouds,—
A corner, warm water—
Hears a tapping—
Legs, shorts, socks running—
Sitting on the lowest step, the grapes—

Oak leaves and early spring clouds,

a mirror. One that holds two fitting
in a single blue chair, size as proportionate to
measure and weight. Weight carried,
weight as erroneously believing
frayed corners, in trusting reliance to be
lies in the light. Stairs to the bared
rafters, sun falling patches through webbed
glass and bats nestled, furred wings amid
rust and exposed nails. There was beauty
in the unlined face, racing fear in the grasping.
That it would stand still. That it would be
pale blue paint splattered, boards hauled
under fat grapes sweating sugar, would be
recast and plumbed for a room
as yet to come to exist as one.

A corner, warm water

pouring over his small head, full body
lifting and lowering in air, in a towel
in the fogged glass. A pleasure
in what appears endless being
the fibers of place, this worn, one, this
a physical lifting when an exterior
presence recedes, freeing what pressures
within. The warmth of my child's body,
the shoulder that calms
the fog and shows how to withstand it.

Hears a tapping

under the window. It is perhaps
a branch, a rodent, starting again
to cross the wide lawn, with us
sitting in darkness within
silence, severing bindings, undoing
connectors within shared
ceilings, walls, and remnant dissonance
welding into the short trellises standing
as one does in the bare that this is, ceilings,
windows, a bus shelter, spring
dusk, and a stake.

Legs, shorts, socks running

toward the building and into the sky
the rain bloats. Shy leaves in
cloud cover, fabric and framework,
tears into wine boxes, wind, and wet
streaks on bare arms. The heart heft,
weight, heart and his tears and thin
calves hover stranger. Behind us,
with us, within our rooms
filled with smooth stones
and seasons, colors and teeth.
Structures and salt licks,
cleared underbrush, wood chips,
four-square, bent wire, chalk and blind
light. The building three stories and brick,
stuffed mended animal bare spots
clutched under his arm. Staples piercing
bright letters, with baskets for done
and undone.

Sitting on the lowest step, the grapes

heavy overhead, weeds splitting the concrete
and the time allotment we are, the unmarked moments
falling asleep amid stuffed toys,
frightening a small child who fears waking
won't come. The quiet, the sunlit
limbs, shoulders, the alley in daylight.
Wet shirts venting in slow steam and a tree
over a bench covered in pale moss.
A sparrow overhead on a wire
that is passed pain, dryness at the crook
of the mouth, where the lips meet.
The bright in having been is a magnolia
where snow once stopped falling.
A hand plunging down into a fishbowl,
a single fish frightened then freed.

If this is it, this season shrinking

rough seams. If the last worked and hewn
word will be, I'll say: let it be brightness. Let it
petal-cast our homes. Let it say I saw
you and couldn't, for the ice emerald season
warming sweat streaking collarbones, I
pulled tight to stand straight beneath
beauty in the building, trunks on the sky as they
were, berry and burned-been. If this: I couldn't
look but for the barreling trains and
afternoon sunlight. A kindness in the south
-facing windows shows where the water was: knows
each crease there, afternoon, boy and babyhood.
Fresh to the warm rails, the smell of them.
Our corner familiar, cut stalks, familiar, did.

Dust dried on the warm porch steps:

pink sun, knots in, and I see
how any one of us here,
a decade or so on, holds this in. Is hurting
self-done, as self-in, as self- what to say
next in the dark that is holes to trip into,
dimensional dark, muted heart and hair drawn.
The term is to lead, to lead on, to
ease. If not to test. If not to we did, climbing grapes
clinging the fingers. Pleasant, then not.
Then not in the realm
of eradicable. Of the talks and stalks and is in
fact something to stand up. To stand on.

A matter of scale,

the afternoon together.
I imagine we have built the landscape
as one can, fingers setting rock by rock,
etching neat furrows of greenery.
What is it that we, we want
to see. Peaked blue
mountains pressed to rise
where in the distance from this room
someone might climb, or might
remember having done so.
The landscape melting as one
can, the encroaching orange
wheat, sunlight, or flame.

Acknowledgments

“driving darkness: a telestich” appeared in the *North American Review*’s Open Space
“A matter of words” appeared in *The Iowa Review*
“The dreams with a hand hovering above” appeared in the *Paddock Review*
“Wakes, stumbles the haze out of” appeared in the *LEON Literary Review*

sample.spring was prepared with support from the Beahl and Irene H. Perrine Faculty Fellowship at Coe College.

Thank you, David Hamilton, Jan Weissmiller, and Gina Hausknecht.

Thank you to my family, friends, mentors, colleagues, and students.

This collection is for Miles.

Margaret LeMay's work was a recent finalist for The Iowa Review Awards and has been shortlisted for the Four Way Books Levis Prize, the Marsh Hawk Poetry Prize, and the Finishing Line Press New Women's Voices Award. Poems have appeared in *Another Chicago Magazine, Better, Brink,* the *LEON Literary Review,* the *North American Review, The Cortland Review, The Iowa Review,* and elsewhere. Her writing has served as title and movement titles for a piano quintet commissioned by the Library of Congress. She teaches poetry and creative writing at Coe College.

www.ingramcontent.com/pod-product-compliance
Lightning Source LLC
LaVergne TN
LVHW090541110826
845146LV00003B/1215

* 9 7 9 8 8 9 9 9 0 3 6 1 8 *